## More Sky

Joe Carrick-Varty is a British-Irish poet, writer and founding editor of *bath magg*. He is the author of two pamphlets of poetry: *Somewhere Far* (The Poetry Business, 2019) and *54 Questions for the Man Who Sold a Shotgun to My Father* (Out-Spoken Press, 2020). His work has appeared in the *New Statesman, Granta* and *POETRY*. He won an Eric Gregory Award in 2022. *More Sky* is his debut collection.

Also by Joe Carrick-Varty

# MORE SKY

# JOE CARRICK-VARTY

CARCANET POETRY

First published in Great Britain in 2023 by
Carcanet
Alliance House, 30 Cross Street
Manchester, M2 7AQ
www.carcanet.co.uk

A CIP catalogue record for this book is
available from the British Library.

ISBN 978 1 80017 301 9

Book design by Andrew Latimer
Printed in Great Britain by SRP Ltd, Exeter, Devon

The publisher acknowledges financial
assistance from Arts Council England.

# Contents

*for the stayers*

## And God said

Every time a horse lies down in a sunlit field
an island goes up off the coast of Alaska or Peru
or in the middle of a lake south of Stockholm.
Every time a whale is born albino
a man doesn't die of liver failure and every time
it rains at sea a child speaks first words.
Every time you watch the football
in your alcoholic father's flat
on his little settee that unfolds into a bed
in case you ever wanted to stay
a forest disappears and a doorbell rings.
Every time the ref blows the whistle
and your father boils the kettle and somewhere
islands are going up and oil rigs just watching.

## Sambas for Christmas

In a corner of some far-flung town
on some moon of some planet
at the edge of some pocketed galaxy
the soles of my father's new trainers
are landing on tarmac, squeaking
as they take off again, box-fresh
at the end of his faded black jeans.
They will squeak for a week or so
and then he will die on his back
in his sleep like Jimi Hendrix
after a night at a pub that's not quite my local
whistling as he stumbles home
running his fingers through a rosemary bush
awash in the chippy's neon blue.
Believe, for a minute, that I am not a son
who buys trainers for his father
but a molecule of gas inside a star
whose light still touches a city
that's not quite Oxford where a father
who's not quite mine tries on pairs
of Adidas, Nike, struggling with the laces,
the incomprehensible bow.

## Dear Postie

If no answer please leave parcel behind rhododendron—
if storm hits and rhododendron blows away
please leave parcel inside wheelie bin with brick on top—
if crying baby can be heard on approach
tap three times on bottom-left panel of shed window—
DO NOT ring doorbell—if rainbow windmill
spins slower than usual open phone and call alcoholic father—
if rainbow windmill stops spinning at any moment
come back in month with picture of alcoholic father
eating fish and chips in park—if phone rings out
wait for nesting swallows to return from Africa
then call again—DO NOT mention alcoholic father
to friends colleagues woman you love—DO NOT
kiss woman you love—DO NOT eat sleep
shit watch TV until alcoholic father is spotted
leaving Tesco with Guinness and Hula Hoops—
DO NOT I repeat DO NOT drive to 24-hour Shell garage
spend following afternoon outside alcoholic father's flat
old ladies watching—bay windows blue with Countdown

## When he waits at the bar my father's brain is miles above his pint

like the swimming pool
I watch six cranes
lower onto the roof
of a skyscraper as
my father gets drunk
with a man called Gary
the kind of drunk
you can peer into
their earrings glinting
their hearts a pair of
tiny red whales
I watch the builders
fit three whole floors
with windows
one guy comes out
carrying a fox
dangles it Michael Jackson-
style over the lip
of a balcony my father
cannot remember
the name of the film
the score of the game
sometimes I drink
and lie and tell strangers
in pub gardens
that my father
is being built that
he's coming back
from the ground

that I'll pull a fox
out of his body one day
carry it in my arms
blinking and pissing
to a sunlit table
just like this one

## Withdrawal

Unpack tins of soup—open windows—
scrape grease from the hob—
sync your breathing with his—walk
with purpose between the bathroom
and the light-filled kitchen—
find a moth and let it live—postcards
in a drawer—pictures of a holiday—on the carpet
build a house out of tins—a family—
trees dotted around a pond—
a swallow's nest like the backdoor of a star—
a note on the table you'll soon cycle away from
your fingers like prunes and smelling of bleach

## Five days sober and glowing

the dad sips a lime soda in the same chair at the same table by the same window at the same distance from the same screen in the same view of the same bar in the same pub on the same street with the same school by the same river on the same bus route in the same city with the same Christmas in the same country on the same island in the same hemisphere in the same trainers with the same son

## THE CHILDREN

on the muted screen a ball lands
one side of a line
and this means that a person has won
the camera jiggles
zooms out refocuses on a crowd
who are cheering
which means that a person has won
yes clapping
back smacking drink dropping
all signifiers
that yep a ball has landed
one side of a line
one side not one side but ONE
SIDE of course right
because a person has won
a ball has landed
people are happy and although this is not
a metaphor for grief
I cannot deny that a ball not a ball but
THE BALL
has landed is landing will land
until it stops being
THE BALL and starts being a ball
at the edge of
a roofless room lots of people are
jumping around in-
side of lots of sound lots of screens
lots of open sky and
did I mention my dad has taken a
shotgun to a field
and I haven't realised because I am
watching tennis
which means my dad has decided
is deciding

will decide to become not a dad
but THE DAD
is asking a man for a shotgun is
saying can I buy
yes bring me this much and it's a
man from the pub
someone I'll walk past for years
which means I am
existing in relation to this moment
my sister is
eating a choc ice romping around
the garden holding
a toad in relation to this pocket of
time my mum
zipping up our puffer jackets pulling
down our hats
while my dad walks through rain
to an ATM
leaves a room with a shotgun in a
duffle bag
this moment almost encased in
glass
this skyscraper I am not really watching
tennis inside of
not on my lunch break not
twenty six
but nine years old being pulled out of
maths
my sister four whole years
barely taller
than a table and we are not children
anymore
but THE CHILDREN THOSE CHILDREN
THAT CHILD

## The Minotaur

*1. Six Lies*

The Minotaur tells his sixth lie of the day
to a colleague, seventh to the bus driver,
eighth to himself as he pays for a Twix,
smiling down at the woman behind the till.

His ninth he tells to a pooing dog,
tenth to its shadow, eleventh to its walker
who nods gravely, opening a pink plastic bag.
The Minotaur finds a bench by a fountain

and there he unwraps the Twix, promising
as he peels away the shiny paper
that he won't eat chocolate again for a month.
A man in a suit and six o'clock stubble is asking

where the nearest train bridge is and *are they frequent?*
In the corner of the room the radio speaks words
like rips of Velcro. The Minotaur pads the landing,
golden wrapper rustling in his pocket like a bird.

## 2. *All the Devil's Mess*

Because this is any other Saturday
the Minotaur is walking his invisible dog
in the park, clumping through snow
towards the iced brown pond

where the quilted backs of silver-
haired men huddle at the jetty, whizzing
their remote-controlled boats
across its island of melt water.

Because this is any other Saturday
the Minotaur is unsheathing
a tennis racket and ball. He's winking
at the men, his eyelashes lined with snow.

This evening, in a pub's dark corner,
hear them whisper of horns, of a bark and a ball
and boats lost and ice snapped like chipboard,
of a pond folded once, like a table.

### 3. The Moon

The Minotaur is convinced he has swallowed the moon.
He googles *irrational fear of moon swallowing*
and walks the park at night looking up at the moon,
touching the spot where he knows

the real moon is lodged. A baby on the tube
pokes the moon in his throat
and the Minotaur's flinch short-circuits
the carriage lights, makes the baby cry.

The Minotaur tells this story to Dr Reynolds,
swallowing it deeper and deeper with every word.
Have you ever tried throwing up the moon?
On his 40th birthday the Minotaur lifts the moon

from its place above the dusty paperbacks.
He pockets it, takes it swimming
the following day with his six-year-old daughter,
forgets the moon in a café one afternoon, tells no one.

## Suicide is not your dad and your favourite rapper going for coffee

(although that would be cute) eating bits of your own mouth eating bits of your own mouth in the queue at Morrisons in the park staring at a baby staring at a big group of people your age kicking a ball back (nice!) the thrill you feel the ball actually going where you want it is not suicide your dad and your favourite rapper are at this stage getting on a treat (of course) you could bottle this you think the collective glow of their shoulders sell it call it suicide if a room of dead dads and a room of dead rappers fell from the same height which room would reach the ground first take a walk wheelie bin cherry tree magpie bicycle how could suicide exist here bay windows so steamy so breathed on

## Perhaps Here Both Our Guiltlessness
## Becomes Clearest

*After Franz Kafka*

A gives B a piece of advice
that is frank
in keeping with his attitude to life
not very nice but
even today perfectly usual
in the city a piece of advice that
might prevent damage
to health this piece of advice
is for B morally not very
fortifying but why shouldn't
he be able to work his way
out of the damage in the course
of the years and anyway there is
no reason for the advice itself
to cause B's entire future
world to collapse around him
and yet something of this kind
does occur but only because
A is you and B is me*

A punches B in the face
on a family holiday
in Portugal the act of which
although inherently violent
is made truly violent by
what follows ie the game
they are here to watch together
which just so happens to be
the centre piece of the holiday
and all the happiness
that must now happen
and does still happen
not in spite of the punch
but in light of the punch
as B holds up a flag for a photo
as A brings a hotdog
as the stadium empties a sigh
and a pair of smashed sunglasses
watch the sky from a bin

*The left side of this poem is taken from *Letter to Father* by Franz Kafka.

## A week and not a word since the argument

I'm cycling near your block,
cycling for no reason, to nowhere,
but I'm near your block, on your road in fact,
passing the Baptist Church
and the redbrick half-finished new build
and in no time at all the shape of you is walking towards me
slap bang in the middle of the road.
We talk, albeit gingerly, about my work at the playscheme,
about the kids who fight there,
about my sister off to Uni in a month—
*to Glasgow! As if she could've picked a further place.*
You slur only a little when you say that.
*Where you off anyway?*
*Nowhere.*

The barman you call Mason nods,
unlocks the side door, props it open,
motions you inside. I look at my watch: 11 a.m.—
I'm seven years old, waiting with a Coke outside
the frosted glass of The Seven Stars,
smelling cigarettes every time the door bangs—
then I'm you, in Dublin, your father
at the bar, more hair than the both of us, taller
in the backlit glow of the doorway
than I'd known him from the black and white photo
you stuck to the fridge one Christmas Eve.
You gather us around, whiskey-whisper *this is your Grandad,*
no liver cirrhosis, not dead at 48,
still bringing pork scratchings and a bottle of fizzy pop
to land with a clink on the step.

*So, you coming in or not?*

## If you chained yourself

to the top-most seat on the top-most tier of Wembley Stadium and one drop of rain fell on the centre circle, then two drops, then four drops, doubling every minute, how long would it be before you drowned? Twelve hours. So that last minute, the last of the seven hundred twenty, eleven hours fifty-nine, the second before that last minute, how full would the stadium be? It would be half full. At eleven hours fifty-nine the water would be fifty metres from your throat. It might resemble a swimming pool or a lake with ripples, yes, plastic bags, a reflection of the sun, a flock passing, then the wind might hush, that sun disappear, traffic on Rutherford Way or Falton Road might stop, look up at the ocean emptying out of the sky, think I hope nobody's in there.

## All my fathers are hunting dodos in the park


and I'm watching through an attic's round window
as one of my fathers, dressed in balaclava
and green camo, commando-crawls
across the tennis court while another

crouches behind a wheelie bin, whispers
to himself, cheek paint smudged,
a grenade clutched to his breast.
Gun fire across the boating pond.

Bullets rip the water. One of my fathers
has broken his leg, snaps a branch
for a splint. Another has climbed a tree.
An explosion and a wheelie bin goes flying.

I ask myself if hunt is even the right verb.
I have never seen a real dodo
and neither have any of my fathers.
No, my fathers are killing my fathers in the park

and I'm watching through an attic's round window.

## The Father Heavens

*After* Buddhism *at the British Library, 25 October 2019 – 29 February 2020*

### 1. *Father Cosmology*

This cosmological map depicts the heavenly
realm called 82a Wytham Street with palaces, gardens
and marketplaces for the 33 fathers who reside there.
In the middle is the settee of the father
Daniel who is lord of this heaven. See
the hot rock hole, the ancient shape of a backside.
Take a seat. Oh, you've done that before.
This is one of six heavens or celestial realms.

## 2. Fathers of Previous World Cycles

In the *Theravāda* tradition, four fathers are believed
to have attained Nirvana. The history of these fathers
is given in a text which is traditionally read
to sons in the bath. Kukusandha father
(top) is the first father, Koṇāgamana is the second
father, Kassapa is the third father and the
historical father Daniel born as Our Prince Danny
is the fourth and final father of this era.
Every father has always achieved enlightenment
in the shadow of a certain tree.

### 3. *Great Peacock Wisdom King*

This manual contains paintings of altars for
sons who will one day become fathers
and may end up alone in a flat or may not.
One father can be seen riding a peacock, a bird
that keeps a territory free from snakes. Can you spot
the note left three years ago saying *I've hoovered*?
Yes, a faint smell of skin and Hula Hoops. On the right
a father appears in a stylised wheel. Between
the spokes are the names for certain kinds of shadow.

## 4. Life Father

Fatherhood is described as a series of manifestations
that are impermanent. It is thought that there
is no ultimate reality in things—every father
is subject to change and to some extent
dependent (dep / en / dent) on perception.
Sonhood does not encourage
belief in a creator deity or
supreme being. However, where
have you walked to this Sunday morning?
Get up from this settee. Close that empty fridge.
See the years of letters at the door?
Gather them up.

## What if suicide is just taking off your headphones

*After Gboyega Odubanjo*

said the blue whale to the lemming
I think you need to take a walk said the lemming

but I've been walking all year
last week I was in the Arctic watching an ice shelf

the lemming regarded the blue whale
did you know glacier water is blue

because it contains no oxygen
stop trying to change the subject

glacier water contains no oxygen because
in glaciers the pressure causes air to be squeezed out

increasing the density of the ice
the blue whale creaked like a train

a glacier lake appears blue because
it absorbs other colours more efficiently than blue

that doesn't really explain anything said the blue whale
the lemming sucked teeth

I'm only trying to gee you up
the blue whale remembered being a chubby year 7

asking Emmy Strachan out over text
my arms are T-Rex arms my hands are open peaches

the lemming considered telling the blue whale the anecdote
about its family who jumped off a cliff

in a Disney documentary but instead
the lemming cupped its palm to the blue whale's nose

and held it there for a few seconds
then the lemming kissed the blue whale's cheek

which for reference was the size of a church window
so the lemming had to stand on tip toes

and like that the pair became best friends
and the blue whale promised to carry the lemming

on its back wherever they wanted to go
and this is how islands were made

## The brick

is chipped and lying on the street before it becomes airborne before it becomes an object capable of flight the brick is clay and water rock weathering on a hillside sediment on a lake floor in Coventry my Irish family sit down to dinner behind a window sky rains robin perches evening happens to the brick chipped in all its glory no longer a piece of wall not snug the brick one perfect handful on account of my family's Irishness my dad's mixed accent got him kicked as a kid my dad Irish in Coventry English in Dublin touches the badge on his chest my knee when we tells me

## Somewhere Far

Walking back from nursery
down Cornmarket to the shop on Ship Street,
*You wait our here now* and then a pen,
one of those little blue ones,
*draw me something nice,*
betting slips, twenty of them.

And when I'd finished the first batch
out you came with more,
*Very nice* and *I like that one,*
maybe a Refresher or two.
Men passing on the step
smiled or nodded or shuffled

but mostly they said nothing
because I was as much a part of that place
as any of the footballers on the walls,
or the fruit machines, or the commentators,
or the screens where you would stand

when you thought I couldn't see,
*Don't come in, you mustn't come in,*
tapping your foot, hands in pockets,
face turned up at the horses
making their way from left to right
across the green light of somewhere

far from here.

## More Sky

Have you ever had that thing when a building
gets demolished, a building you walk past every day,
a big but inconspicuous building,
a building you've never properly looked at,
couldn't draw from memory, guess
its number of windows, the impression of a building,
the colour of sandstone in your periphery
as you hurry into afternoons, interviews,
wedding receptions and all of a sudden it's gone,
there's sky where that building used to be
and you're a mess with your child's bike helmet?

## Lop Nur

My father dives headfirst into a lake,
swims till his pink shoulders become stars.
He swims for days, beach to beach.

The pink shoulders of my father's stars
are attached to other stars by invisible rope.
Birds perch on them. Cranes and gulls

and bony blue herons appear at 6 a.m.
from behind the mountain, slipping
like moons, more the more you look.

My headfirst dive's no match.
Feel the gulp that's coming, barnacle-
chinned, the birds inexplicably lifting.

## Moonless June

For weeks they arrive out of the Arctic Ocean,
watched by a grizzly momma and her cubs,
my father in a sky blue suit,
long sideburns, Elvis Costello glasses,
my giggling sister on his shoulders.
For weeks they cross the beach. For weeks
they reach the treeline, my sister
an old woman and my father a baby
swaddled in the suit. She rests for breath,
leans her one free arm against a boulder.
The cubs have stopped noticing—momma drinks
from a stream, paws at the moonless water.
My sister drops the suit, hears it land, breathes
like a woman I have never met.

### When you lean close and tell me

not a day goes by that you don't think of him
but you're thinking less now and you hope this is a sign
I pick at the grass and remember all the people

I've thought about since this conversation started—
an ex from school, Sylvia upstairs, the postie.
When I exit the roundabout behind an ASDA lorry

it's not the A342 Northbound I'm driving on but the
freckled curve of my father's spine. When a stranger
spots them from the layby, points a gloved hand

to the horses drinking from the lake of my father's face
I climb the field to get a better view. In the valley
two leafless trees fill with light, become lungs.

## Parks

*For Caitlin*

For the hour it takes to write this poem
I'll believe the pigeon in Brookes library
is my father's mind, back for a weekend,
delivered to my sister and me
in the shape of his face, his beanie hat,
the quick glint of his silver earring.

My father's mind hides in plain sight,
waving from a picnic bench in a busy park,
his perfectly timed smile a trick of skin—
another afternoon of swings and slides.
I believe the pigeon is my father's mind
because no one else has spotted it

perched up there on the light fitting, cooing.
If I have it right, if I know our father,
the pigeon will be gone by morning,
ushered out by some cleaner. And then
for the rest of the week the bird is nowhere
and everywhere we look.

## 54 Questions for the Man Who Sold a Shotgun to My Father

Is tea an exact science / Are willow trees categorically sad / Can a house have a face / Are astronauts real / How many bad things have been witnessed by just deer / Is hiking peaceful / Are skyscrapers pretty / Was there an imposter at the wake / What does flamingo taste like / Are bees kind / Is the BBC right / Do lemmings understand / Are children who lose a parent to suicide more likely to die the same way / How many kettles are whistling right now / How many tractors will break down today / What did the first nectarine smell of / Where are all the dead ducks / Do whales dream / How many Boeing 737s have successfully landed since 2002 / How old is the oldest tree in Alaska / Which shade of orange was your son's bedroom this morning / How many rivers are there between my body and yours / Is stilton your favourite cheese / Have you ever been to Budapest / Do you have an opinion on Coldplay / Do you remember your ninth birthday / Do you fly well / Do you burp more often than you think you should / Are you hairy / How many mugs have you dropped / Have you ever stroked an elephant / At what age did you stop believing in Santa / How many weddings have you attended / Do you enjoy French films / Have you ever been operated on / Is your garden south-west facing / Do you own a pair of secateurs / Would you call yourself a family man / Were you ever any good at tennis / Is your penis longer than mine / Does it rain in your weather / Is there a bus / Are you waiting by the frozen fruit in Aldi / Wearing a beanie / Listening to U2 / Did he tell you what he wanted it for / Did you ask / Did he smile / Did you touch / Talk much / Had he shaved / If you could us a number to describe his laugh would you use 1000 or 3 / Did you put the money towards a loft extension / Is that a lasagne in your oven?

## Panasonic RF-P50DEG-S

they
must
have
known
more
than
they
let
on
the
birds
you
would
probably
laugh
both
hands
deep
in
your
pockets
and
looking
up
as
you
do
because
hey
I've
got

this
radio
I
can't
give
you
and
there's
a
wheel-
barrow
in
my
garden
full
to
bursting
with
feathers
I
didn't
ask
for

## Draw a circle around the city you grew up in

look / the field you lost your virginity in / isn't far from the field your dad stopped breathing in / isn't far from the field he taught you how to ride a bike in / isn't far from the field normal families (which included yours for a while) used to picnic in / isn't far from the field he coached your football team in / isn't far from the field he watched you play cricket in / isn't far from the field you smoked your first cigarette in / isn't far from the field your ninth birthday went well then went wrong in / your tenth birthday went well then went well then went wrong in / your twelfth birthday went wrong in / isn't far from the field other families went quiet in / isn't far from the field a few birds lifted from the trees in / isn't far from the field your mum refused to remove her sunglasses in / the restaurant / parents' evening / even at breakfast in her dressing down her coffee smoking her lip only slightly puffy

## You are always the last to know things

like how suicide will grow
from a seed
from a chilli your dad
bought in Tesco
like how he will use the end
of a sharp knife
to remove suicide
instead of frying it with garlic
like how he will fold
suicide between two pieces
of paper before adding
turmeric to the rice water
like how he will check
on suicide at 4:21am
like how a fox will
watch him do this
like how he will arrive
unshaved and puffy
one morning
with a small pot
like how this will mean
you have inherited suicide
the same way your body inherited
bad knees and baldness

like how lawnmowers
can propel grass
with three times the muzzle energy
of a sawn-off shotgun
like how a sawn-off
shotgun can fire a bullet
through the engine block
of an aeroplane
like how there's a company
in Arkansas that will
turn your loved one's ashes
into ammunition
like how ammunition
fired into the air
almost always
falls back at terminal velocity
like how the odds
of being injured or killed
by an accidental firearm discharge
are 1 out of 6509
like how a bullet can travel
for so long the rotation
of the earth
will move the target

## From the Perspective of Coral

*An exhibition in seven rooms*

There are a large number of particulates suspended
in the ocean, and while suicide does not
have eyelashes to keep particulates out of its eyes
as humans do, it emits a certain frequency
(some call it a hum, a toothache,
the background wind of a 4am voicemail)
which continuously bathes the eye
with an oily protein mucous.

Considered one of the least-known
and rarest living things, suicide
is hardly ever seen with the naked eye

except last week in Morrisons when
reaching for a mango, opening
a box of eggs
to check for cracks.

Suicide needs to see
in a wide range of light levels.
Anyone who has gone scuba diving knows
the difficulties of underwater vision.
Visibility can be affected by the turbidity of water
and the deeper you get
the less light penetrates and you slowly
lose colours.

I'd like to draw your attention to slide 7
'Suicide Suspended', as seen from the ocean floor
(from the perspective of coral).

It is unclear as to whether suicide is ascending
or descending. It is unclear as to whether
suicide is alone or calling to a mate.

I'd like you to imagine the deepest,
widest body of water you can.

I'd like you to hold this water in your mind
the way you might an auntie or pet.

I'd like you to call this water your water.

Now, please fill out this short questionnaire:

Is it night or day in your water?
Would you call your water a friend or an enemy?
Has your water ever been taught how to float?
Does your water remember a particular holiday in Tenerife?
Does the sight of your water make your nose itch?
Do hospitals sleep in your water?
If your water could talk, would it be kind?
Would its voice be deep or high-pitched?
Does your water have its own mythology?
What is your water's favourite season?
What was your water's first thought this morning?
What was the last thing it drowned?

Suicide vocalizations are the sounds made by suicide
to communicate. The word 'song'
is used in particular to describe the pattern
of regular and predictable sounds
made by suicide in a way that is reminiscent
of a human singing.

See, for instance, this pizza-eating example
(resident of England some 26 years).

See how it wears shorts in the park in summer?

See how it makes plans to visit Japan with a friend?

See how it chews sugar free gum? Pays rent?

Here it comes...

Don't breathe too hard!

Would you look at that... making small talk with the bus driver!

Remarkable... simply remarkable.

Suicide plays hide and seek with a human diver

Suicide disappears behind the hull of a sunk ship

Suicide (blushing) is a terrible flirt

Stop it! For crying out loud stop it!

(canned laughter, spatters of booing)

Suicide slinks off stage left

Crouches at the other end of the ocean

## Some Dads

*After Emily Berry and Wayne Holloway-Smith*

A colony of dads / Six football pitches of dads every week for a year / A spoonful of dad / A dad the size of Sweden / Thirteen fully grown dads off the coast of Mexico / Clippings of dad / Dad on the softies: window seat, ice in his drink / This recipe will contain one whole dad / Two-pint dad: inquisitive, sharp / A dad with treasure inside / Evidence of dads confirmed by NASA / This-is-going-to-hurt-a-bit dad / Six miles as the dad flies / A dad's beanie / A dad-shaped thigh bruise / Four-pint dad: fun, beneath the flatscreen TV / Schrödinger's dad / Slow dad / Slurry dad / They-got-my-medication-wrong dad / 'Dad's flat smells' / Long time no dad / Saturday morning dad: every creak like a storm breathing / Six-pint dad: likes to play-fight / 'Dad needs new trainers' / A dadventure / A dadvent calendar / A dad viewed from the round window of a submarine / Eight-pint dad / Ten-pint dad / Twelve-pint dad: 2pm on a Tuesday / A childhood of dads at the school fete, fighting / A dad on his doorstep / A dad in a poem / Wafer of dad / Stomach of dad / Seizure of dad / The cycle of dads: tomato soup, sleep / Dad on the softies: window seat, ice in his drink

## / dream in which /

*For Caitlin*

he uses a shotgun and
we are relieved if a little shocked not at
the fact he did it or the field he chose or
the shoes he was wearing or the day of
the week or the dog walker who finds
him / dream in which / we are shocked
at how relieved we feel spreading
marmalade onto too-hard toast the
dog's name happens to begin with the
letter P how about that / dream in which
/ we headshot our nanna on Christmas
Eve before anyone finds her in the bath
correction before he finds her before he
lifts her / dream in which / we murder
the letter P we brick every window every
silhouette every cosy family every game
of scrabble every sentence with the word
perfect or Peter / dream in which / we
wait on the landing with a shotgun as
our nanna does her thing because we are
not here for her we are here for him
and she knows this she's even left the door
ajar a slice of light / dream in which / we
murder Christmas so Christmas can
never go wrong so nothing can be found
inside the turkey the stuffing the
adjacent room we leave spiders in the
chimney poison ivy on the roof / dream
in which / we wear balaclavas to shoot
up the bath shop in town we shoot a
store clerk who's older than George
Burns we shoot every taloned white ball

claw every inch of marble / dream in which / he is scampering up the carpeted stairs all eight years of his body no bad thing to find no razor just light across the estate little brothers little uncles bunkbed asleep he is the oldest boy in the world / dream in which / we murder the idea of waiting for something to happen we murder the waiting we murder the happening we murder the years / dream in which / his chest explodes on the top step one hand on the banister and we let him see our faces his foetuses / dream in which / our nanna is pregnant in Coventry she is fresh off the boat she is sixteen and crossing the road outside a pub NO BLACKS NO DOGS NO IRISH (we murder the sign) / dream in which / we murder her brain her freckles we murder 300 butterfly eggs the wings they would inherit / dream in which / we run up on the boatman at Dublin docks the ticket inspector the neighbour who helped with the luggage we leave their entrails on the beach then we shoot head-sized holes in every boat this side of Ireland / dream in which / we torch 700,000 blades of grass 76 willow trees 63 benches 800 bird boxes we build a bonfire out of nature trails and kissing gates and kingfishers and stag beetles and red squirrels and blue lambs we cook sausages we tell scary stories we dance in the morning we are naked we lay down in the white coals

## In Amber

In my dream you are almost drunk,
struggling with the lock on the french doors
of my childhood, a lit cigarette
cupped in your palm.

Seconds before I wake, I realise
I've no idea which side you're on, which side
of those huge lime-scaled sheets of glass
you huddle to, hunched and cursing

the key which catches as you turn it. Sure,
the garden lurks behind, the gravel path,
but so does the television, the empty fish tank,
the cat's water bowl. So, which side are you on,

and where does that leave me?
Give me a clue—nod, blink, catch my eye,
crunch a snail shell, ash your cigarette,
flick the butt so I might hear it land.

If I could reach I'd pluck a silver hair from your arm,
just one, like a dream's very own pinch,
a dream we'll both wake from, at the same time,
on the sofa, some film playing ... *Did you feel it too?*

## The Secret

You only smoked at midnight
the back door ajar
moon in the bevelled glass
a tap footsteps the latch. Some nights
I could hear meteors from my bed
and still the television CNN
the muffled fucks or a cough
every boom and crackle
of every crater opening up in the carpet.

Yes it rained one morning
when I asked *Dad what's lithium?*
and you bolted then re-bolted
the kitchen window.
I might have believed lithium was a small bird
or a smell that glass couldn't keep out
or in.

## Supercalifragilisticexpialidocious

It happens next summer when the car in front turns left
at the motel sign and a doe notices just in time
to blink and a man with a bag of beers looks
but doesn't slow any.
Or tonight, when I wake
to your naked arm cold and too heavy
so my breath holds as I pretend not to feel, pretend
I didn't catch its eye and, for a second
consider braking left
on a year I'm yet to live. It happens
on a bridge over a train track, a father back for a weekend, a son
propped on the railings
arms in a V, altogether unaware of the light's red to amber,
the freight around the bend, its horn
an impact that will whoosh through him, keep him
quiet all the way home
up there on his father's shoulders.

## My father is sitting on the other side of the french doors

just sitting, like a grizzly bear I shoo away in June.
Back hunched, staring at the ground, a red biro
tucked behind his ear. I like to think
he's marvelling at the patio we dug,
the pebble path I skipped school to help lay,
or planning for another pond, another
row of sunflowers by the wall.
                                        Right on cue
the cat arrives and figure-of-eights a plant pot
as my father itches the back of her neck with the biro,
flicks greenflies from his shirt.
I can never wake early from this dream,
never sprint fast enough down the landing, never
unzip the blinds, swing open the window in time to hear
the thud of his footsteps over the shed roof,
branches bouncing back to stillness. And I'll never know—how could I?—
that in this dream he'd grow old, grow fur, eventually.
The locals think I'm crazy
they say you shouldn't feed the bears—*dumb Brit*.
They say a grizzly will return for a lifetime to the spot
it once found food, the exact kink of river,
stubby bush, overflowing garbage can
but I do it anyway, always at night, barefoot, in case
he comes, my father, sniffs me out,
calls off this silly game, crosses the Atlantic, Canada
and I'm already gone
he'll see my shoes tucked behind the glass,
laces in a bow,
and he'll think no different—he'll wait, he'll sit,
back hunched, staring at the ground,
till August ends and the bears, wide-eyed,
come for him too.

## Lamech

I ask my father to die under my breath
in the back of a cab on a Saturday afternoon
traffic at a standstill both ways, the pair of us
heading for a cinema like normal people.
I ask the driver to take us back. Back to the pub?
I shake my head, begin to name things
tree car cloud streetlamp, pull my father down
onto my lap, stroke his bald head
look I say a park children are playing
listen I say it has started to rain.

## Ode to Shotgun

O feather duster O scatter O devotion O misfortune's repeater O ogre's boomstick O thirsty carbon O timeworm O tribute O whisper of accidents O blunderbuss O mighty mouse O lighthouse O primitive silver O shadowmoon O oblivion, voice of the harvest O sucking straw O prophecy O skyscraper O echo bone O slipping slide O epilogue O fusillade O requiem O peppershaker O lap dance O due diligence O smoky buster O Gov'ner O rain O rain falling O rain falling on the stillest lake that was all of our futures

## There's a Person Reflected on the TV Calling Their Dad

The seagulls are circling, calling their dads,
the rain is calling its dad and so is the sun
and what's left of the lawn, a skyscraper
is kneeling and calling its dad, a bus, a train,
a city is calling its dad, the mouth
of an underground station opening, Halloween
has called, Christmas will call soon enough
and that new year climbing over the back wall
through the screen door is, of course,
calling its dad. I stand in a room and call my dad,
tell his answer machine not to worry anymore,
that they have found his body.

## Sometimes I Talk to Myself as if I'm on a Chat Show

which is to say I've followed him somewhere
I shouldn't have which is to say alleyway broken glass
foxes all over the bins and all I can think is where
are his trainers he must believe we do not love him
walking barefoot through a neighbourhood like this
which is to say he isn't coming back which is to say
moon like you wouldn't believe which is to say
without blood on his feet and a lot of hobbling
he isn't coming back dad ffs we have three options
here but let me tell you the fourth option
STOP WALKING TOWARDS THE SEA I will not
stand for this I will not whisper I will not wear face
paint and a plastic sword and follow you gladly
we all know what happens

**sky doc**

Once upon a time when suicide was a thought

        folded inside a thought folded inside

        a thought folded inside my dad's

        breast pocket at the edge of the reef

        every member of my nuclear family

        lies down nothing wrong with the water

        they say it's fine to breathe just watch

        then suicide pulls up slow as a planet

Once upon a time when suicide was a whippersnapper

        snap snapping at our heels my mum

        wore sunglasses four days in a row

        in December the sky with no bruise of its own

        when we went to the park I could tell

        the other mums kept touching their eyes

        the water being fine to breathe I decided

        to kill a beetle drop its body down the slide

Once upon a time when suicide was planting beans

in a dark cupboard and I named my bean Felix

around the time I realised my family

was probably very wrong was when

I started going for sleepovers I think

I dropped a bowl and nothing stormed

from the edge of the reef from the edge

of the bed suicide switches the sun off

Once upon a time when suicide was the decision to drink

500ml of celery juice every morning

on an empty stomach or the decision

to walk in one direction for a year

in order to avoid certain patterns

of thought suicide is so close we can

smell its lavender breath my sister

takes my hand links her fingers

Once upon a time when suicide's favourite bird was a

robin because they are sociable

and will follow you down a path

at a safe distance I remember the

holiday in Tenerife I made friends

with a boy called Robin who had

terrible sunburn blisters where are your

parents boomed my dad from the balcony

Once upon a time when suicide was a cardboard cut-out

family in a museum somewhere north

of this reef people came from miles

to stare at a safe distance I remember

one summer a football tournament

my dad marched me home because

I didn't make the A team tried to fight

the coach everyone in the field stared

Once upon a time when suicide was a year filling

with slow increments of awful picnics

another birthday squashed flat fossilised

my mum in sunglasses again I think

we were out for a curry no one talked

cheering a few metres from the reef is suicide

how long do we have to watch

not long now croons the coral

Once upon a time when suicide was the notion that time

is the best healer my dad in the garden

stuffing his body with sky I was sixteen

before anyone told me anything

my dad chased me out the house

in his favourite blue sweater I remember

in the park I bumped into a teacher

where are your shoes she said

Once upon a time when suicide was the butterfly bruise

      that happens to the sky

      when a nose gets broken the slow lakes

      that pool and the four stages of colour

      suicide slow dancing with my mum

      under spotlight even the fish are impressed

      I want very much to make a father

      of suicide to climb inside and sleep there

Once upon a time when suicide was the greatest magician

to ever spend a night in my treehouse

in the 90s I wanted to die

before anyone told me about my family's

mythology my hereditary a procession

of beetles heading for an ocean

for a second I'm Micky Mouse in *Fantasia*

suicide will be home from work soon

Once upon a time when suicide was wearing my family

       like the pink end of a sunset and we queued

       round the block just to break a piece off

       outside the cinema my sister offered me

       a bird's wing and 1/8 of a cloud

       her hands full of pomegranate seeds

       and diazepam pills suicide promises

       to smuggle me home a piece of sun

Once upon a time when suicide was the slow shape

of a blue whale coming up to breathe

in a David Attenborough documentary

my mum in some happy act of resistance

asking us to dance to Pet Shop Boys

in the living room before school

we danced for two songs before

my dad stomped on the ceiling

Once upon a time when suicide was a cat called Oscar

who died for three weeks my sister

assembled a feast of things he had

never tasted I remember watching him

drink double cream for the first time

standing under the cherry tree

where we sprinkled Oscar's ashes

was the first place I saw my dad cry

Once upon a time when suicide was a forest I planted

and instead of trees grew every person

I ever hurt packed into a school hall

on a Tuesday all of them wearing

colour-coded socks depending

on the degree of hurt I have caused

suicide asks on a scale of 1-1000

how sorry do I feel for myself

Once upon a time when suicide was a red taxi

with the metre running and I couldn't

find my tennis racket have you ever

attended tennis practice having been punched

twice in the back of the head

the ball goes up the ball goes down

the other kids have names like Lois

and Conor their t-shirts smell of lavender

Once upon a time when suicide was the simplest way

of saying honey please take the bins out

like many kids the first person

to punch me in the face was my dad

like many dads the first person

to punch him in the face was his dad

and so on and so forth until suicide

is busy painting a smile on the moon

Once upon a time when suicide was the weather

in my mum's suitcase an entire

departure lounge of silent meteorology

a few metres from the reef suicide

is giving the best team talk ever

I remember my mum handing over

our passports removing her sunglasses

we saw her eyes for the first time in a week

Once upon a time when suicide was the safest thought

in my boathouse of safe thoughts

as a kid I would open the skin

at the top of my thigh every time

my dad hit my mum I would bury

a pebble in the garden to think

of those pebbles so safe

surrounded by all that soil

Once upon a time when suicide was the best collection

of Disney videos this side of the park

as for happiness my body

understood being happy

in increments of danger

how much damage could I do

to master this feeling we watched *Mulan*

my friend Jake had the quietest dad

Once upon a time when suicide was the difference between

the body as fruit and the body as labour

between beach sunshine in the movies

and beach sunshine in the 90s

when the contents of my family

would travel a long way to deflate

on a picnic blanket play happiness

hiding in plain sight maybe we looked believable

Once upon a time when suicide was being diagnosed with

asthma instead of OCD in the year 2003

aged 9 my body already overthinking

its most basic function suicide carries out

CPR on my family while simultaneously

giving a lecture on blue whales did you know

blue whales are conscious breathers the sound

of my body forgetting how to breathe

Once upon a time when suicide was proof I was busy living

the day my dad took a shotgun to a field

I watched 4 hours of tennis

I would tell you the last thing he said to me

was honey please take the bins out

but I would be lying so strange

to put words in his mouth give him

honey instead of a bullet

Once upon a time when suicide was an empty street

and we ran until our lungs hurt

in order to weaponize a child

within a family dynamic

a parent must use violence and affection

in equal measure I remember my dad

broke my nose with the flat of his hand

all weekend held onto my sister so gently

Once upon a time when suicide was rain on the lake

the very smile my sister would pull

when she was a certain kind of afraid

it was hard for us to be friends as kids

owing to the way our dad bounced

from one to the next I think

if you saw us back then

you would guess we were happy

Once upon a time when suicide was a magpie

finding the remains of another magpie

to tell you the truth we have no idea

what other people are thinking

back on the reef suicide has adopted

a soft northern accent facts about my 11th birthday

my dad punched me in Sports Direct

I pissed myself the cashier was lovely

Once upon a time when suicide was a Venn diagram

with the word battle in the middle

what a stupid word to describe losing

your dad's favourite blue sweater I once

wrote a letter to my sister apologising

for things I knew I hadn't done

is it worse to watch the violence

or have the violence done to you

Once upon a time when suicide was being the hero

of your own story hey look

this awful thing happened but I'm OK

I'm still here I'm even writing something

beautiful to be honest I'm a survivor

to be a survivor implies there are others

who didn't make it out alive which of course

is true suicide asks about my sleep

Once upon a time when suicide was the sky

above a demolished building

and I could never make my zip work

my friend Libby described an experiment

in which light behaves differently

depending on whether it is observed or not

alone in my bedroom I was king of zips

ruler of zips nothing scared in the mirror

Once upon a time when suicide was not the least bit romantic

one Christmas my nana ran a bath

and never came back my dad had this plan

to visit Thailand something

about a turtle he had seen on TV

like wishing the film would end different

for the longest time I believed

he had gone to find the turtle

Once upon a time when suicide was walking the lip

of the volcano they say insanity

is doing the same thing over and over

and expecting different results

can this relate to patterns of thought

if you think about dying enough

but you wake up again you brush your teeth

you put on your dad's favourite blue sweater

Once upon a time when suicide was a lark in a poem

and I went down to the lake

where my dad was last seen

alive by a dogwalker called Sinéad

at 9:30am one Tuesday in May

I pulled away some brambles

I lifted a log

I was very hungover

Once upon a time when suicide was the closest thing

        I ever saw to a polar bear

        an albino badger on the college playing fields

        my dad drunk before I understood

        what drunkness meant

        for everyone else in the vicinity

        I would learn not to ask for sleepovers

        for example I would learn quickly

Once upon a time when suicide was an open-top bus tour

and my sister climbed the sky for a dare

meanwhile suicide has turned itself

into a nesting doll it unzips

and another one steps out I remember

I missed English third period

my sister hooked up to several machines

my mum at work in a different city

Once upon a time when suicide was grinding its hoofs to nails

to what extent are we the same

as our thoughts a theme park of my loudest

explosions as a kid I would wake up

convinced I had burned the house down

my mum bringing me back to earth

with a pebble on my cheek my dad

offering Starbursts could be so gentle

Once upon a time when suicide was the belief

that everyone in the cinema

could hear the back of my throat

suicide has baked a tiered cake

tall as a skyscraper

my sister chooses the elevator

this decision taken out of context

means very little

Once upon a time when suicide was a GP who told me

I was just overthinking everything

it's funny how much damage

people are capable of the person

capable of the most damage

never said a thing like that to me

perhaps my dad most of all

understood where we came from

Once upon a time when suicide was the vaguest direction

in a world of vague directions

I have wanted to die

in most fast food outlets

suicide spins a globe tells me

anywhere you like I remember

being on a nature trail for the first time

in years felt like going home

Once upon a time when suicide was another word for sorry

a blue jacket in the middle distance

cutting into the treeline I wonder

if my mum cut a dash in sunglasses

at parents' evening maybe the teachers

thought her a rock star have you ever

marked suicide on a map in green felt tip

blink once for yes twice for no

Once upon a time when suicide was a room of dead dads

and a room of dead rappers

falling from the same height

do you understand what I mean

when I say family is climate

holidays were always the worst

in beautiful places my mum in sunglasses

like every other mum

Once upon a time when suicide was a bull in a china shop

two elderly tennis players

touching fists between points

trainers poking out from behind a bush

I was pulled out of maths

offered a custard cream

and a special chair in the bright office

my sister already waiting

Once upon a time when suicide was the verb to gloam

to begin to grow dark to grow dusky

during picnics perhaps we smelled off

a few metres from the reef suicide

is shadowboxing to rapturous applause

the sky shakes a bird loose my mum

the challenger bears her gumshield

like her life depends on it

Once upon a time when suicide was too proud

to be hurt into words I remember

the holiday I realised nothing

is a puzzle unless it comes in a box

a volcano is not a triangle

more a succession of steepening hills

but hey that kid with a blue face at breakfast

probably ran into a door

Once upon a time when suicide was getting everything I need

then I'm gone but it's not stealing

violence and all the self-harm that lilts

boys will be boys someone said

when we lined up on that hill

overlooking the city maybe

we had come to finish our fathers

maybe to finish ourselves

Once upon a time when suicide was say the magic word

and uncle T will appear I once

opened the door to my dad's middle brother

having not seen him in two years

he looked pink it was bonfire night

my dad hanging a Catherine wheel

recounted to a neighbour his brother

on our doorstep full up on class A

Once upon a time when suicide was a rational phobia

of nature trails and trying to explain

to uni friends that a tent can be a body

in the right light sometimes my dad

would fight other dads in the street

one holiday in Rome for example

by the time they were finished

neither dad had any shoes on

Once upon a time when suicide was the realisation

that being scared is caused mostly

by thinking on the topic of thought

keeping close to the walls suicide

assures me it has the perfect analogy

imagine your sister's body snorkelling

outside of its life now keep imagining

whatever you do don't forget

Once upon a time when suicide was an infinity pool

with panoramic views and I wasn't brave enough

to open my eyes underwater

until the morning of checkout

heading for a taxi fully clothed

I took the plunge suicide with megaphone

is holding a protest who knows if I saw

what I needed to see in that water

Once upon a time when suicide was a cat called Minnie

who could hardly lift her head to drink

but on the day of her choosing

climbed the shed then disappeared

forever my dad long gone

would have called her a dark horse

in need of something to bury

we planted a rose under the cherry tree

Once upon a time when suicide was not where you're from

but where you pay rent the first time

I was excluded from school my dad

promised the belt over the phone

in the headteachers' office

that stern woman maybe she guessed

my head nodding

my mouth saying yes sure OK

Once upon a time when suicide was plagiarising birdsong

I might add that my dad never used

the belt on me his violence

like his love was hard to predict

the first time I was excluded from school

we watched *King Kong* I remember

outside the cinema he knelt down

zipped up my jacket in the bright sunshine

Once upon a time when suicide was a choice of two smiles

of course I had friends who were beaten

for punishment the violence they described

always sounded so organised four smacks

on the ass or come here open your hands

then slap to me it sounded civilised

pain you could predict

and in turn prepare yourself for

Once upon a time when suicide was scaffolding for the sky

all the silence the countless times my dad

slammed the door forever after a row

with my mum have you ever heard a house

exhale for the duration of a weekend

just the cats padding the landing

my mum smoking cross legged on the lawn

when she stood again how tall she looked

Once upon a time when suicide was the answer to the question

when a tree falls in my forest of memories

and no one else hears it has it happened

suicide purring wants to know the answer

to a different question tell me

if a room of dead dads and a room

of dead rappers fell from the same height

which room would reach the ground first

Once upon a time when suicide was choosing the wrong friend

to be honest with at a house party

in year 11 and how that friend

not my best but certainly not my worst

never quite looked me in the eye again

on the topic of always saying too much

suicide pulls up a plastic patio chair

envelopes me in the booziest hug

Once upon a time when suicide was rain that gathers

and protects its own darkness

I told my mum I believed

I was a murderer she was

coming out of the toilet

of course believing and being

are two different things suicide

pockets a star promises me unlimited wishes

Once upon a time when suicide was two schools of thought

       the borderline heroic tried very hard

       couldn't take it anymore

       or the selfish but how could you

       someone would have to find you

       the best way of explaining suicide to anyone

       was a drawer I opened one morning

       full of my dad's old elastic bands

Once upon a time when suicide was an hourglass

tipped on its side that old cliché

about love and knowing

where to look what if I told you my dad still

crosses the street some Sundays

wearing the same Helly Hansen

his body stopped breathing inside of

and always it's me he doesn't recognise

Once upon a time when suicide was a hole in the sky

through which my family landed

suicide sifting for gold has found

the perfect river if I stand at the bank

and look to the east I can make out

the shape of my dad walking home

after a weekend of radio silence

I watch him feel the house inhale

Once upon a time when suicide was an Irish uncle

who Facebook-messaged me to say

you are not and never will be Irish

suicide measures me a thimbleful

of torrential rain I never reply

to my uncle but sometimes

I scroll to his message and see him typing

three dots but he never hits send

Once upon a time when suicide was another dream entirely

my dad walking out of the ocean

in a sky blue suit long sideburns

my giggling sister on his shoulders

for weeks they cross the beach

for weeks they reach the treeline

my sister an old woman

my dad a baby swaddled in the suit

Once upon a time when suicide was the most glowing

characteristic the presence of lava

being the sole difference between

a volcano and a mountain and how

this speaks nothing to the empty

stadium that's been going on and how

a volcano viewed from the sky

must look like a mouth saying O

Once upon a time when suicide was a storm that stripped

comparison from the landscape

a therapist once likened my sadness

to a tree's collection of year rings

back on the reef my sister trudges in

from the field her body both alike

and not alike her sadness which I feel

coming on some nights several cities away

Once upon a time when suicide was anointing my family

with special hats in honour of our

collective having made it so far

the ceiling of my nursery

was painted blue with a beaming sun

for what it's worth in dreams I sometimes

take my family down to the beach

where it rains but we finish our picnic

Once upon a time when suicide was an auspicious debut

my sister crying very quietly

in the back of a cab versus my sister

graduating from uni

like a person on Instagram

from the back of the auditorium

my dad who never gets to see this

booms her name turns every middle class head

# Notes

This book borrows and/or paraphrases material from the following sources:

p. 22: Franz Kafka (*Letter to Father*).
p. 30: Gboyega Odubanjo ('A Story About Water').
p. 51: Emily Berry (*Dear Boy*), Wayne Holloway-Smith (*Alarum*).
p. 52: 'store clerk who's older than George Burns'—Eminem, Dr Dre ('Guilty Conscience').
p: 98 'grinding its hoofs to nails'—Terrance Hayes (*American Sonnets for My Past and Future Assassin*).
p. 106: 'too proud to be hurt into words'—Mimi Khalvati (*The Meanest Flower*).
p. 107: 'getting everything I need then I'm gone but it's not stealing'—Mac Miller ('Good News').
p. 110: 'being scared is caused mostly by thinking'—David Foster Wallace (*Brief Interviews with Hideous Men*).
p. 113: 'not where you're from but where you pay rent'—Outkast ('ATliens').
p. 117: 'when a tree falls in my forest of memories and no one else hears it has it happened'—Kathryn Harrison (*True Crimes*).
p. 119: 'rain that gathers and protects its own darkness'—John Ashbery (*Houseboat Days*).
p. 126: 'a storm that stripped comparison from the landscape'—Shane McCrae (*Sometimes I Never Suffered*).

## Acknowledgements

Thank you to the editors and staff of the following publications where some of this work—or versions of it—first appeared: *Anthropocence, Banshee, Granta, Ink, Sweat, and Tears, The Interpreter's House, Magma, Manchester Review, New Poetries VIII, New Statesman, PN Review, POETRY, Poetry Ireland Review, Poetry London, Poetry Shed, The Poetry Review, Prototype IV, The Scores* and *The Tangerine*. Thank you to The University of Manchester's Centre for New Writing, The Society of Authors and Arts Council England for generous support. Special thanks to all the people who helped—in so many ways—with this book, specifically: Rowland Bagnall, Eve Esfandiari-Denney, Elizabeth Garrett, Vona Groarke, Wayne Holloway-Smith, Andrew Latimer, John McAuliffe, Gboyega Odubanjo, Michael Schmidt and Mariah Whelan. Never-ending love to my family.